Creamy C...

A Book of Irish Poetry

By

Sydney Mc Shane
&
Cathie L. Mc Shane

Creamy Celtic Cake
A Book of Irish Poetry

For information and permission, write to

Creamy Celtic Cake
Celtic Nations Art
c/o Cathie or Sydney McShane
P.O. Box 20673
Fountain Hills, AZ 85269

Or

e-mail: **creamycelticcake@yahoo.com**

Library of Congress Control Number: 1-792-554
ISBN - 13:978-0615676883
ISBN - 10:061567688X

Dedication

This book is dedicated to

Kathleen Lee.

Acknowledgements

Thank you to:

My mother,
for making me follow through on my education
and for her unconditional love and patience.

My grandfather,
whose own love of poetry inspired my own.

My teachers,
for encouraging me to write.

My friends at the Irish Cultural Center.

My daughter Cathie,
for editing my English
and for her contributions to this book.

My beloved Kathleen,
for always supporting me.

Table of Contents

About the Authors

Sydney McShane was born on August 18, 1936, in his family home in the wee town of Lurgan, Northern Ireland. He is the son of an Irish weaver, a job which, in the mid-1900s, provided his family with a bit more than a farmer's pay would allow. Nevertheless, they lived humbly in the home his grandfather had built with his own hands, and they gratefully shared what they had with the families around them.

Sydney was a cheeky child, dreaming of going fishing in the nearby trout stream or taking apples from Knox's farm, instead of learning his lessons at Sunday school. Still, Sydney was very close to both his grandmother and mother, who taught him to love and not to hate those who were of different faiths or backgrounds.

At the age of 16, Sydney's first job was as an apprentice in the Johnson and Allen Linen Factory, where he learned how to repair sewing machines. Sydney felt unsuited for this task, and so, he became a painter's apprentice. Since wages were too low, at one pound per week, Sydney and a friend went to Bristol, England, where wages were five to six times higher than in Northern Ireland. From there, he went to America and joined the U.S. army at age 21. The military provided him both the order and the discipline needed in a young man's life.

Honorably discharged two years later, Sydney attended Bible college. After graduating, Sydney married and became a minister. Just six years later, he brought his wife and two daughters, Caroline and Cathie, to Phoenix, Arizona. Sydney found work as a painter and wallpaper hanger but also ministered throughout the state on Sundays. He had two more daughters, Cheryl and Michelle, who also love hiking and fishing with their father.

Besides his love for his family, one of Sydney's greatest passions is hiking. At the time of printing, Sydney is retired "but not tired" at 76. He still hikes nearly two miles every morning. His morning hikes inspire his poetry and landscape paintings. Both hobbies he developed a few years ago when he first retired. With the encouragement and support of his wife, Kathleen (now deceased), Sydney began and continues to share his impressions of the desert southwest, as well as his unique perspectives on Irish culture, history and blarney.

Cathie McShane is Sydney's co-author, as well as the editor of this book. She was born on the east coast of America, just a couple of years before the family headed west to Arizona. Since then, she has spent all her life in Arizona.

After graduating in the top three percent of over 700 students in her class, Cathie attended the University of Arizona, where
she received her degree in teaching Spanish and a minor in English. After several years of teaching, she earned her master's degree in educational leadership from Arizona State University. This year marks her 26th year of teaching for the Mesa School District in Mesa, Arizona.

Cathie currently resides in Fountain Hills, Arizona, with her cats Oushka, Indy, and Sparks. One of Cathie's passions is training animals. Both Indy and Oushka are leash-trained and can respond on command and perform various tricks usually associated with dogs. Oushka is being trained as a therapy pet to visit the sick and home-bound, and Indy will be trained for agility competitions. Additionally, Cathie volunteers for the Nine Lives Foundation, serving in various capacities and as a foster home for their cats and kittens.

Introduction

Ireland is a land of myths and legends, of truth and imaginative half-truths. My love for folklore and history began with the stories my grandfather and father and would tell me over and over near the fire. On roadside chats with the old folks, they would tell tales which, I still think, they believed to some extent. When I began working, many men would share the stories they knew, with their own twist on the facts. In Ireland, the facts are, undoubtedly, embellished, since this form of entertainment is still an Irish tradition. The superstitions, too, like the cry of the Banshee, mix with facts.

Many of the poems in this book follow this tradition of my homeland. At times you will find yourself believing every word. After all, getting caught up in the possible is what enjoying an Irishman's stories is all about. Like Irish folklore and legends, "Leprechaun Food" is a poem for amusement, while "God's Promise" will touch the heart.

My poetry is influenced by my personal experiences growing up in Ireland before the modern conveniences and other influences of the 21st century and by years of living in the Arizona desert. As a boy, I spent most of my time outside, wandering through the fields, walking along the trout streams, and fishing under the old stone bridges. I loved to read practically anything I could get my hands on. My favorite poem was by James Mansfield, because he wrote it while he was in the Glens of Antrim looking out at the sea, something I would do, too. His impressions of the sea and the sky are breathtaking.

Even today, I love the outdoors, not just being outside, but being away from the city and enjoying nature. During my morning hikes with my Welsh corgi, Pippin, up the mountain preserve near my home in Phoenix, we often come across coyotes, snakes, and big horned owls. The desert itself is vast and awe-inspiring, especially the old saguaros.

I cannot end this introduction without acknowledging my daughter Cathie's contributions to this collection of Irish poetry. She not only edited this book, but I also asked her to include a few of her own poems. I've told her that they're "not quite right," but then, nor is her father. As we Irish would say, most of us are "missing a brick on the chimney" anyway.

To you, dear reader, enjoy and God bless.

Creamy Celtic Cake

Cliffs of Moher

Located along the south-western coast Ireland, the majestic cliffs of Moher rise high above the sea and are some of the highest in Europe. The morning mist and fog make them appear to be wrapped in a soft blanket.

O Cliffs of Moher,
you are the lore
of fifty thousand Celts
and more.
Wispy morning clouds
grasp and hug
your highest cliff.
Upon your rugged face
they stay and gently kiss.

Cold Atlantic waves
dash upon your ancient,
eroded rocks below,
putting on an audible, classic,
perfect picture show.
Wildflowers, grass, and shamrocks
grow upon your placid top,
spreading profusely far and wide
and seem to never stop.

Celtic maidens
love knights of might
and armor bright.
They dream of them
all through the night,
but to all of us,

you are that brave
and charming knight:
We behold your handsome face,
strength, and awesome height.

O Cliffs of Moher,
we Irish Celts adore
your pristine beauty,
unmatched along the great Atlantic shore.
Forever, may we look and see
your mighty cliffs
rising above the raging sea.

Soothing Rain

Growing up in a cottage without electricity or running water is an experience that few can appreciate today. In the cottage, only there can you appreciate life in tune with nature - no videogames, television, phone - nothing to distract you from enjoying living the simple life.

Moisture from heaven graciously sent:
the gentle, soft rain of Ireland, a welcome event.
Look through the cottage window
and see the spring flowers,
and the robin in the budding tree tops
seems to sing every hour.

Walk out the cottage door and down the wee path.
The soothing rain on your face you'll want to last.
Ireland's spring rain, the essence of nature, behold,
and with the help of God's sunshine,
new life shall unfold.

Old Dan McCann

The Irish are known for their gift of the gab, as well as for stretching the truth a wee bit. Children often gather around their grandparents to hear stories of Irish legends - stories passed from generation to generation - and as they are passed, the truth is stretched just a wee bit more each time.

Old Dan McCann,
from the banks of the Bann,
he greased his hair
from the frying pan.
His teeth were pure black.
'Tis truly a fact,
and when he spat on the ground,
he turned it all brown.

He cooked in a pot
and ate all the fat.
True, none of us
would do anything like that.
Then, he fiddled and played
his tunes oh so sweet,
for single young ladies,
he did want to meet.

But he died an old bachelor,
as far as we know,
never kissing a maiden
with teeth white as pure snow.
So, on the banks of the Bann,
among the reeds and the sand,
they buried the old legend,

old Dan McCann.
Up in heaven,
the bachelor's hands softly play
the tunes that he fiddled
each evening, each day.
Here we laugh and remember.
His story is told.
An old legend of old Ireland,
o let him be so.

Fishing Father

Many of Christ's disciples were fishermen, but Christ called them to be the fishers of men. Many priests and ministers fish for relaxation, and some become very good and can compete with the best in the world. Some say that Father McVay was among the best.

In the Irish town of Athlone,
Father McVay was well known.
He fished in the great rivers,
wee streams, and cold lakes.
With his own hands,
black flies he always did make.

Each misty or clear day,
the father fished all alone.
Along the long, mossy banks,
he often liked to roam,
but he never complained
nor gave out a loud groan,
although it was quite hard
on the old father's old bones.

He traveled to the states
to visit a long-time, good friend.
A triumphant message over there
he wanted to send.
He fished along the Snake River
in Washington State,
and his legend soon grew
at a miraculous rate.

Some say the father's fishing secrets
went by the grave,
or perhaps, they are still hidden
in a Donegal cave.
Today, the fish in the waters,
from the States to Athlone,
are safe and contented,
because they're left all alone.

From Heaven, Father McVay
is looking down
at those fish in the river,
with a grin and a frown,
and in the markets,
his fish are not to be found,
'cause fishing Father McVay
is no longer around.

Irish Hillbilly Man

When I last visited Ireland, I met a man that fit the picture of people I have known in the hills and mountains of America. Their ways, their talk, and their dress all seem to be common factors. As this man would say, "all a hillbilly requires is his daily needs not his greeds."

In the soft, rolling hills
of west County Down,
I was fortunate to meet
an Irish hillbilly man.

He spoke with his accent,
hillbilly rich and hillbilly smooth.
His eyes, they did twitch.
His ears seemed to move,
yet with his soft voice,
a crying child could be soothed.

The hat he wore looked like
his dog had it for lunch,
'cause it sat on his head,
all crinkled and crunched.
His trousers and shirt
he washed in the river
and dried on the rocks.
I didn't ask him,
but I'm sure
there were holes in his socks.

He lived in a wee meadow
with hills all around,
and near the trees in his meadow,

was a small still on the ground.
Around his wee home,
the grass was beyond tall:
for a bandit or thief,
a good place to hide from the law.
Piles of trash were scattered
where he did dwell.
In the summer time, it would have
a horrible smell.

This hillbilly's neighbours said,
"He acts as dumb as an ox,
but underneath,
he is as sly as a fox.
He can build homes and mansions
from the floor to the roof.
Look around the countryside;
you will see the full proof.

A hillbilly welcome awaits you
when you knock on his door.
He is loved by his neighbours,
grandchildren, and more."

I asked to take his picture,
and he did agree
but said, "If I include my two ducks,
it will cost you a fee."

There are hillbillies the world over
who are as nice as can be,
and this one from County Down
left an impression on me.

Cathedrals of Armagh

Armagh is Ireland's ecclesiastical capital. It's the seat of the Roman Catholic Church and of the Protestant Church of Ireland. In the fifth century, Saint Patrick founded a church here on the site of Fort "Ard Macha."

In Armagh city, two cathedrals stand,
looking down on this
divided
land,
both lovingly built by Celtic hands.

Of different views they are, you see,
but just one God they serve,
and one truth shall be,
which is he died to make all of us free.

Their doors are open to us all:
the weak, the strong,
and those that fall,
and from their pulpits,
they preach no hate
to those who wish to congregate.

Within their walls, we love to hear
those songs of love
and not of fear,
and as we look towards their spires,
may God's peace be
our only desire.

May Ireland be the land they see,
of peace and joy and harmony.

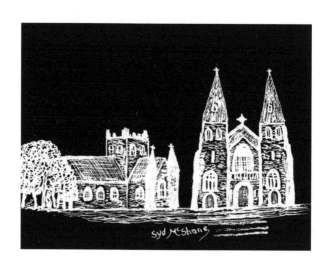

O Leprechaun, O Leprechaun

Leprechauns are very wealthy and are known to hoard their gold. Some claim that if you follow a rainbow, at the end, you will find a leprechaun's pot of gold, but no one has ever found one, because the rainbow fades too fast.

O leprechaun, O leprechaun,
I know where you hide:
'tween the cracks in the granite
on the green mountainside.

Your jacket's too small.
Your shoes are too tight.
Your hat just won't fit,
and that I'll admit.

I'll seek out your gold
and steal it away.
A mansion I'll build
on a hill far away.

But maybe I won't,
'cause stealing's not right,
and I'm not quite ready
for a leprechaun fight.

So, just give me a buckle,
a smirk, and a pat,
and ol' Ireland and I
will be thankful for that.

The Irish Cottage

The history of the Irish thatched-roof cottage began with the Irish peasants who built them with stones from the nearby fields, and the roofs were thatched with wheat or barley straw. They used willow saplings to hold the thatch down. The cottages were whitewashed with ground limestone from quarries.

In whole the world,
there is no cottage as warm,
built with such pride
or so full of Irish charm.
With walls of fieldstone
and roof thatched with straw,
we look upon her with grace
and with humble awe.

Around the stone fireplace
is the gathering place.
It makes both family and stranger
feel warm and truly safe.
The aroma that comes
from the burning black peat
will make you linger,
to stay, and not want to retreat.

The stranger can come in
and sip some hot tea.
The Irish spirit and true love
he always shall see.
The glowing peat fire
warms the loft high above,
where the children sleep
with peace and with family love.

The parents sleep nestled
together below.
Maybe they hear the winds
that howl and blow,
but they know they're protected
from every harm,
because around them
are God's gentle hands
and strong arms.

May the warmth of every Irish cottage
always thus be,
in our lives and in our hearts,
for whole the world to see.

Leprechaun Food

Leprechauns often seek out the same food we eat, but be careful: they use their own special spices, which could make us mere mortals more than sick.

Leprechaun food is delicious
but somewhat suspicious.

With mushrooms from Kerry
and cabbage from Derry,
they make grasshopper stew,
which they season with brew.
This recipe is known to only those few.

If they find a wee hen,
they will cook it right then,
and when it is done,
put it on a leprechaun bun.

At one o'clock sharp,
if you hear the dog bark,
they're prowling around,
some eggs to be found.
There'll be no sales at the fair,
if they find them right there.

When the sun goes down,
they will hide in the rocks
and empty sour berries
from out of their socks.
They'll sit down and snack.
Then, it's off to their beds,

all quite full and well fed.
Yes, leprechaun food is delicious
but also so very, very suspicious.

Sinkable

In the story of the Titanic, which I believe to be true, it has been told that, on the day of the launch, a priest walked by the great ship and saw where someone had inscribed or chalked on the hull "Unsinkable." The priest turned to the crowd and said, "This is blasphemy! Only God is unsinkable!" As we know, those words rang true.

Down Belfast Laugh,
the great Titanic did sail.
Only God knew
she was destined to fail.
From stern to mast,
she was the pride of Belfast,
but one word was inscribed
with boldness and pride,
calling her invincible,
even naming her "Unsinkable."

An honorable priest
went by the great hull,
and his true words
were specific and full.
"Blasphemy against God,"
were the words that he spoke.
Yes, his message was received
by our common folk.

Out into the north Atlantic
she went,
but the steel on her sides
was soon to be rent.
An iceberg did loom,

and the Titanic was doomed.
Down to the bottom
the Unsinkable went.
Maybe a message from God
really had been sent.

As she lies on the floor
of the vast ocean,
silent and sleeping
without any motion,
let her stay there
in her cold, rusty grave,
because she is the home
of our honorable brave.

The good father
did what he thought was right,
when he spoke his words
with truth and much might,
but in what was to be
Titanic's darkest night,
may we see again
God's divine guidance and light.

Lasting Love

True romance and love between a man and a woman is lovelier than anything else on Earth. This poem acknowledges that a real man can be soft and romantic, and his inner feelings can be as deep as a woman's.

To me you are
a rare, beautiful butterfly.
Just to know your love,
all the world's treasures
couldn't buy.

Your eyes
are more intriguing
than a thousand
cascading waterfalls.
Portraying passionate love,
even sadness,
they tell it all.

Your lips are tender,
like the velvet feel
of Irish moss,
and are always warm,
never cold
like Ireland's winter frost.

Sometimes, you look so sad,
and it makes me
want to cry.
Try to understand:
it's my love for you
that'll never fade nor die.

Wee butterfly,
I feel, sometimes,
you want to go and fly away.
Please don't:
'cause deep down,
I miss and love you more
each passing day.

Your outward beauty
may fade a wee bit
because of Father Time,
but my love for you,
now and forever,
will never waver nor decline.

So, don't go back.
Don't return to your cocoon,
'cause you are precious to me
morning, evening, and noon.

Autumn Splendor

Early autumn frost permeates the crisp, clean air,
but warmth fills my soul from splendid color everywhere.
Songbirds of Ireland sing in the lovely canopy above,
songs I don't understand, but I know and love.

Shades of orange and red with rust and yellow
make me feel alive yet mellow.
Tender autumn leaves flutter gently to the ground
or twist and swirl. So, in distant fields, they are found.

They touch the frigid and frosty earth below,
staying there through winter's ice and snow
or fading and turning slowly to dust,
but I'll remember autumn's yellow, orange, and red rust.

Dublin Accent

How you speak, so articulate.
The words are quite clear.
The English-speaking world
should listen and hear.

Like the sound
of an Irish meadowlark
in early spring,
music to our language
your accent does bring.

Unlike the sharp and harsh
Scottish accent of the North,
yours is more smooth,
like the lovely hair
of a lass, of course.

Oh, people of Dublin,
you sound so unique.
All the Irish are proud
of the way that you speak.

Creamy Celtic Cake

Creamy Celtic Cake contains
carrots, cream, and candy
and is cooked quietly
at Cathie's Celtic Creations,
'cause it causes a commotion
with customers who crave
Creamy Celtic Cake!

Creamy Celtic Cake

Creamy Celtic Cake,
made with words
soft, uplifting, humorous, and divine,
sweetens and nourishes our souls
with laughter every day
when we dine.

Savor words of joy and of peace.
Let them flow from your body
and into your soul,
and your happiness will grow
as much as three fold.

Paddy's Whiskey

In south Antrim,
along the shores of Laugh Neagh,
a small graveyard is famous to locals,
even today.
In there lies Paddy Mulligan,
a whiskey-drinking man,
and right there next to him
is his wee brother Dan.

Seven years after him,
Paddy's only sister, Mary, died.
So loved by the locals,
even the wake priest cried.
They opened Paddy's grave
to place Mary's coffin on top.
"Oh, what a surprise," they say,
"the grave digger he got!"

You see:
years ago, embalming
was only done to a few,
mostly to the rich
and to those who sat in the front pew.
"The whiskey embalmed Paddy
from his head to his feet."
That's what everyone says
at the pub, when they all meet.

Leprechauns and Politicians

Leprechauns and politicians
are somewhat alike:
They both are arrogant, proud,
and verbally fight.
Leprechauns have riches,
an abundance of gold.
Politicians in office?
Their riches - three fold.

Both dress up in the finest of suits,
but there aren't enough pockets
to hold what they steal
or what they loot.

Leprechauns craft
fine buckles and shoes.
Politicians tell lies
and point out their views.

Leprechauns are fluent
when they stand up to speak,
and politicians use fancy words.
Just to figure them out
could take up to a week.

Wee leprechauns, may you never
leave this green land,
but you crooked politicians,
from serving in office,
will be permanently banned.

Grumpy Old Frog

Not far from our home in Northern Ireland was a peat bog. It was damp and the lower parts were always full of water. This is where the frogs lived and had their offspring. At night, we could hear them from the house. They were so slimy from the stagnant, dirty water that we never considered them as food.

Upon a wee log,
in the middle of a peat bog,
sat a muddy, slimy,
and grumpy old frog.
And beneath the wee log
that the frog sat upon,
dirty, slimy water
formed a tiny, wee pond.

Among the reeds
and all kinds of weeds,
other frogs would come there
to swim and to feed.
The grumpy frog would chase them away
by jumping in with a loud splash,
and the loud noise he made
would even frighten a rat.
Then, he would stick out his chest
and let others know
that he was the Frog King,
from his head to his toes.

Now, the grumpy old frog took sick
and was unable to move.
Then, he said to himself,
"I need help! Oh, what can I do?"

Soon, the other frogs
helped him get well
and brought him food.
He was thankful, and he promised
to be grumpy no more,
and he lived to the old age
of six years and four more.

Mr. Fox

Out in the Irish countryside, my home was surrounded by farms. There were many wild animals that would run off with the farmers' chickens, ducks, or geese. The farmers, of course, disliked them and didn't see the beauty of these crafty animals, but I've always had a soft spot for them in my heart. After all, they're hungry, too!

You rusty red fox,
I will seek and will find
your small den.
The reason, you see,
is I think you stole my wee hen.
Underneath the fence,
there's a gaping hole.
You are cunning, brave,
sly, and so bold.

Red fur you left behind.
You are guilty.
You have no defense.
Evidence is plenty.

Now that soft snow
covers the hard ground,
I know it won't be long
before you are found.
Your paw prints I'll trace
until I find your den:
I'll have proof enough
that you have my wee hen.

But I know I'll forgive you
and won't hurt you anyway,
'cause I want see you in the fields
of County Down next May.

The Irish Redhead

Their hair is so beautiful,
so soft, so fine.
Men like to be with them
to dance and to dine.
From the North they come
and from the South and the West.
It's hard to decide
just which one looks the best.

When the morning sunshine
reflects through their hair,
there's nothing in color
or beauty that compares.

They are not just for looks
or to put on a show.
You talk to them politely
and keep your voice low,
'cause their tempers are known
throughout this green land.
When they lose it,
you'll be ground up
like Donegal sand.

She's passionate and loving,
most of the time.
You could marry her,
and things could be fine,
but other women don't
look at her man,

'cause they may feel the full force
from the back of her hand.

Yes, with an Irish redhead woman,
please don't cross that fine line,
'cause her passion becomes red fury
in a very short time.

Father O'Grady

Most people see priests as being very serious and lacking a sense of humor, but many of them often find humor in everyday life and in helping the people of their parish.

Southwest of Belfast,
in the small town of Glenavy,
the priest of that parish
was none other than O'Grady.

Now, the father was well-respected
and loved by all faiths
because of his love for God
that showed upon his wee face.
The groundskeeper for the parish,
a Protestant named Billy Barnes,
was full of Irish wit,
and of course, of country charm.

Well, as the humorous kind,
the father liked to have fun.
One winter's day, cold and wet,
and the clouds hid the sun,
he asked Billy to come in
and with him have a wee nip.
Warm whiskey near the stove fire
they both slowly did sip.

Strong and pure, not one sweet drop
fell from Billy's cold lips.
"How do you like this whiskey?"

the father did kindly quip.
On the father's kind face
he focused his eyes,
and Billy's reply
was none less than a surprise.

"Father, if your sermons
were as good as this whiskey,
you'd convert every Protestant
in the wee town of Glenavy."
Then, Father O'Grady,
he roared and he laughed,
and to keep from falling,
he had to lean on his staff.

On Sunday, he stood before his flock
with a smile and a grin,
as he told of his wee encounter
between Billy and him.

Good Father O'Grady and Billy
have gone to heaven above,
and they are missed by many,
since they were very well-loved.

Michael Collins

As an Irish patriot, Michael Collins only wanted Ireland to be ruled by the Irish. He could not tolerate English occupation. He was a champion of liberty for all Irish. Many people believe he would have been the first leader of the Republic of Ireland.

Michael Collins,
a true Irish patriot destined to lead,
of your fighting Celtic spirit,
the whole world should read.

For the cause of Ireland's freedom,
you were the best,
always fearless and powerful
in the face of death.

Words of truth, hope, and peace
you clearly spoke,
not a single historian
could ever revoke.

For all Irish,
you sought a free
and peaceful life
in a land without political
and religious strife.

You proclaimed
that freedom, at any cost,
would someday come.
The rhythm of these fateful words
beat like a thousand drums.

CREAMY CELTIC CAKE

A vast, civil war
loomed in the North,
approaching all too soon.
You exclaimed a blood bath
would renew old hate
and reopen those wounds.

For freedom from cruel occupation
you fiercely and bravely fought.
The English surrendered
our land and people,
leaving us to our own lot.

But within your ranks there was,
unhappily,
a bit of dissension.
Without delay,
your own men killed you.
No names
were ever mentioned.

According to you, Michael Collins,
all Irish should stick together,
no matter religion,
but to some prejudice radicals,
good news was your quick assassination.

The Shillelagh

In the corner it waits,
handy and ready,
to whack you by the bartender
or even his daddy.
Most Irish are friendly,
but some like to fight.
Just glance at their shillelagh,
and it will put you to flight.

As a famous cudgel
made out of rough, hard oak,
it may be a weapon
when an Irishman's provoked.
Hard and strong,
inside far from hollow,
if whacked with it,
you will let out a bellow.

While at a pub
for a tall pint of stout,
don't mess with a paddy,
because he'll knock you out.
Just buy him a drink
and speak well of his race,
and you won't have that cane
all over your face.

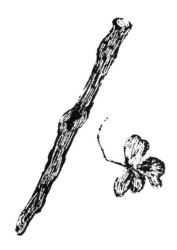

Beyond Despair

To my wee daughter, Cathie, with unquestionable love, I dedicate this poem. May you never again have to face cruel tragedies.

Night seems like day, and day is like night.
There is nothing clear, defined, or bright.
It feels like you have lost your inner sight:
so dark, nothing in your soul is right.

Despair. It shows upon your sweet face.
Its root cause only you must retrace.
You feel you are alone, and no one cares.
"Why me, God? Don't you understand?
It's more than I can bear."

Others might blame you
for the despair you're going through,
not looking to yourself
to see the stronger, inner you.
At times you cry and sob and weep,
and your thoughts to yourself,
you want to keep.

But in the midst of all your grief,
be still and hear God's voice again,
and it will sound like soft, springtime rain,
pattering on an Irish cottage window pane,
and your inner, spiritual strength you will regain.

Love's Identity

What is love?
Does it depend upon the eyes and tongue?
Oh, no. Because perception and speech
cannot carry on so deep
and betray true love
for no more than a sweet whisper
from burning lips.

Does love require fingers entwined
and footsteps side-by-side?
Oh, no, even still!
Love endures beyond the grave
and touches 'evermore,
leaving a imprint
that cannot be washed away.

And the heart, guardian of the ages,
forever man's ideal?
Is it she?
Oh, no, my dearest.
She is fragile, and once broken,
herself never again.
But love, stronger than every beat
of every heart, cannot shatter.

What, then, is love?
Reveal its genuine nature,
so that I may find it for us all!
Ah, sweet friend.
at last you have discovered the truth!

Celtic Roots

Since to a common culture all of us belong,
let our Celtic roots be deep and be strong.

We can sing and dance and write and play,
from the Scottish highlands
to the Galway Bay.

Though of different faiths we are, you see,
our roots belong to the same family tree.

Ireland's Fairies

Without question, the myths and legends of Ireland are some of the best in the world. Sometimes, it is good to get out of the real world and into a world of make believe. Is it possible there are real fairies? Perhaps this poem will help you decide.

Down in the soft, green Antrim Glens,
the fairies hide in their wee homes,
far away from mortal men,
but when the full moon comes out,
they play right there,
without a doubt.

If approached by mortals,
they seem to vanish away.
To where they go, I just cannot say.
Along the steep banks,
near a small waterfall,
tiny footprints can be found.
That tells it to us all.

Their music and laughter
are part of these glens,
and their right to be Irish,
I always will defend.

On a clear, moonlit night,
in those soft Antrim glens,
listen and hear,
oh dear Irish friend.
Their music,
soft and joyful they'll play,

and the fairies will dance
right into the day.

Scottish Thistle

Working on the farms surrounding our house, I grew up thinking that Scottish thistle was no more than a weed that was full of sharp leaves surrounding the flowers. Often, I would prick my finger on them while working the fields, and frequently, we had to remove them from the dogs' paws. As I matured, I saw the beauty in the thistle's tiny purple flowers.

O thistle,
You are close
to every Scottish heart,
loved for your flowers
and deep green leaves,
'though you are
prickly sharp.
Whether in sunshine
or mist or morning dew,
your brilliant purple
has the most perfect hue.

Down the glen
or rugged mountainside,
untamed, you're Scotland's
own natural pride.
Scottish winds
and North Sea gales
can't blow you down.
Sturdy, strong,
you grasp the Isle's
hard, rocky ground.

Some say you are nothing
but a weed,

but to the Scotts,
a purple flower indeed.

Forever, may
the cold Scottish winds
scatter across this Isle
your soft, fluffy seeds.

Maggie Magee

A lady that lived near our farm was as strong as any farm hand. She could pitch hay, work the threshing machine, and do more than any of them in a day.

Maggie Magee
was as strong as could be,
born near Cork City,
about a mile from the sea.

Being so tall,
she could eat hay off a loft.
She could speak very loud
and looked like the boss.

Speaking against her man
made her angry and cross.
You see: he was no higher
than two stones with some moss.

If you mocked this wee man,
your hide she would tan.
You might even receive
a permanent brand.

So, don't mess with a Cork lady,
like Maggie Magee,
or you will go to the doctor's,
and it will cost you a fee.

Now things could be worse
than paying money like that,

'cause you could very well end up
in a cemetery plot.

The Lagan Canal

The canal systems of Ireland in years gone by were some of the best in Europe. Most of Ireland was linked by canals. Before the railways came, they served a very useful purpose: they transported corn and many other goods.

The Lagan canal
links Belfast with Lough Neagh,
an engineering feat of a by-gone day.
The barges carried Scottish coal
and corn from the States
but arrived at their destinations,
at times, very late,
making the customers and owners
more than irate.

Along the tow path,
horses pulled the great barges
one at a time.
When the horses got tired,
the barge men
would moan and would whine.
So, old Bill McVay
and his wife, Maryanne,
decided to work on a simpler plan.

The pike in the canal
were awesome and large.
Thus, they might be able
to push a great barge.
Bill and Maryanne
fed the fish from the side.
The pike snapped at the food

and made ripples quite wide.

This propelled the barge forward,
and it went very fast.
So, they made better time
from the port of Belfast.

The owners received their goods
well on time.
At the pub, Bill and his wife
would drink and would dine.

You can believe this story,
while others do not,
but it paid for a new home
and steak in their pot.

O Gentle Mist

The mist and fog, so common in Ireland, give you a warm feeling. When you walk in them, you feel that you are wrapped up in a blanket of soft, white wool.

From North to South,
you are the same.
There are no boundaries
in your name.

The graveyard stone
you moist the same,
of those of hate
and those of fame.

You touch the heather
to make her grow.
Her perfumes to the heavens
gently do go.

You hide the white smoke,
from every view,
of those that still
their strong, illegal brew.

But never leave
this Emerald Isle,
for in your midst
we see God's smile.

Irish Whiskey

I do not condone excessive drinking. To make whisky, or moonshine, is against the law. The illegal kind is called "Potheen." It was made for home consumption and, sometimes, for sale.

Was whiskey first made
on this island so green?
Full proof of that
is yet to be seen.

Excuses for drinking
the Irish know well.
In an articulate manner,
to others, they'll tell,
"If you have a cold or chill
or are feeling quite low,
warm up some whiskey
and to bed you should go."

This excuse for drinking
is way over-sold.

Jackson and Grant
were of Irish descent.
Perhaps, they drank most of the time,
maybe even through Lent?

Irish rapport with the public
will never be right,
since they are branded as drinkers
and do like to fight.

Now, there are many Irish
that take a wee nip,
and some leave it alone,
and they can be found from Cork City
to the hills of Tyrone.

School Master Maguire

*About three miles from Lurgan, formerly famous as an Irish linen town, was
Kilmore School an old, country schoolhouse. Master Maguire was the head of the
school when I attended there.*

Some Irish school masters
are known to have a short fuse.
In master Maguire's class,
you listened and never snoozed.

His temper was so hot
it could burn the hair off a rat.
To him, burning with fury,
never say "I forgot."

Your homework was done,
always neat and ready on time.
Yes, parents admired him
and thought his teaching just fine.

If you didn't pay attention
or made faces in class,
he would make your behind sore
with a cane very fast.

The windows would rattle
with the sound of his voice.
You had to stay in his class:
there was no other choice.

Master Maguire is long gone,
and Kilmore School is still there,

but his ghost and his fiery presence
can be felt everywhere.

Country Preacher

This poem reflects the humor of some of the country preachers. It is not intended to put down any religion or to attack the Bible in any way.

There was an old preacher
named Billy McComb.
Across Northern Ireland,
he preached, and he roamed.
'Though he repaired country roads
during the week,
on Sunday, his views of the Bible
clearly he would speak.

In the 1950's,
when television was brand new,
across the country,
outside aerials were in plain view.
To the preacher,
they were the devil
on the chimney or roof,
and he would elaborate
but never show any real proof.

In a certain small church,
Deacon Uprichard sat in the front row.
He never moved one inch
and always kept his head far too low.
Each Sunday, Billy would try
to get him to smile or to grin,
but the poor Deacon thought
to smile, in church,

was a sin.

Once Billy preached about Solomon
having a hundred wives,
and he looked at the congregation
with a toothy, broad smile.
"Ninety-nine too many,"
he spoke with a jovial, loud voice,
and in reference to his dear wife,
he had no other choice.

The Old Saguaro

One day, I was walking in the desert, just north of the city of Phoenix, and I noticed a large cactus nearing the end of its life. Some saguaro cacti have many arms, but this cactus' main trunk was broken, and I felt sad for it. Then, I seemed to be comforted knowing that God knows the beginning and end of all things. Still, I stopped and wrote down what the old saguaro might say if it could speak.

Thank you for coming by.
I have seen you walk
your favorite desert path many times.
Why have you never noticed me?

I stand before you, wondering, and wanting
to speak to your soul.

Well, please do not ask my age,
for that is my secret known only to God.

I yearn to give back to others,
because God has given much to me.
I've had a good life.

I thank God,
because he placed me here,
a quiet sentinel
in this great Sonoran Desert,
privileged to welcome the birds
to build their nests in my arms,
protecting them and their young
from predators and storms.

My roots are almost gone.

My back is broken.
My arms are weak and tired,
but my flowers still blossom.
Even in my twilight years,
my inner self doesn't fade.
I am still a reservoir
for God's love and beauty.

I sense the shadows of death
approaching.
My departure is near,
but look around and behold my offspring.
With God, there are no real endings,
only beginnings.

Please come back
and see me again,
maybe paint me on your canvas
the way you see me,
the way I am?

Big Horned Owl

You perch upon
your rocky ledge so high,
a silhouette of beauty
against the desert's early morning sky.
Your hoot is loud and clear,
joyous to one's curious ear,
but to your prey,
it makes them tremble with fear.

Those eyes of yours,
large, yellow saucers of delight,
beautiful, yet cunning,
seekers of tiny prey at night,
they can penetrate deeply
into the very human soul.
Your glance is arrogant,
rightfully proud, and bold.

Your beak and talons
are an awesome sight,
enough to put your enemies to flight.
You swivel your round head
from side to side
and upon your cheeky face,
is a look stern and wild.

In the early morning
or on the darkest of nights,
your nocturnal vision
gives to you perfect sight.

Seeking your prey,
your perch you leave.
Your vast wings move
with precision and ease.

You are a patient hunter,
until you find your prey.
Then, you swoop down fast,
without any delay.

The Coyote Star

Alone among billions like her,
she shines quietly, fiery inside,
but cool and gently twinkling
in the midnight sky.

As the world spins slowly,
always chasing the sun,
she remains steadfast, dependable,
confident in her position.

Off in the distance,
coyotes panting in the desert heat
restlessly gaze,
drinking in her cool light
that comforts their bodies
and calms their spirits.

Storms begin to rage,
Nature's force unleashed -
unpredictable, unyielding.
The coyotes must retreat
into their cave.
The pounding rain
floods the red earth.

Blinding lightening
and piercing thunder
throw the coyotes
into turmoil and panic.

They cry out, terrified,
begging for their star
to soothe them, to rescue them
from their anguish within.

But she cannot,
because the spinning Earth
has changed night into day.
A brighter star and Mother Nature
stand in her way.

The fierce storm,
more swiftly than it began,
abruptly ceases.

When they no longer hear the wind howling,
and the thunder stops roaring,
the coyotes come out to see,
in the clear evening sky,

The Coyote Star,

as brilliant and comforting
as she has always been
and always will be.

We the Irish

This little island, so lush and green,
to we, the Irish, is more than a dream.
Intruders divided and tore us apart,
but our Celtic spirit will never depart.

Let us not be each other's foe,
since we are all proud Celts, you know.
Ruddy-complected, blue-eyed or brown,
yet still the same: our faith is all sound.

From the shores of County Kerry
to old County Down,
we need no foreign culture
nor to be ruled by the crown.
We have our own roots.
What else do we need?
From the North to the South,
we're from all the same seed.

We must settle our differences
in a peaceful way,
for Ireland to be one, united someday.

Peat Bogs

The peat bogs of Ireland have been disappearing at an alarming rate. Power plants that ran on peat have been one of the causes. Let us save what is left, so that future generations will enjoy their beauty.

In the spring,
flowers are abundant everywhere.
Bright yellow, blue, and purple,
they are so fair.
In the trees, birds chirp
their love and mating songs.
You can listen to them
and smile all the day long.

The soft peat beneath the flowers
is like an ocean sponge,
absorbing the rain and taking in
the dew and the sun.

God-given is the purple heather
that grows on Irish bogs.
Its beauty you can dimly see
through the rain or the fog.
Tourists visit the stately mansions
and cathedrals of Dublin city,
her peat bogs more pristine
than that place on the River Liffey.

The scent of peat perfumes
the air along the road,
but don't dig up all the peat

that you see there below,
'cause it will destroy,
forever, the beauty
you view from above,
placed by God himself for us
to admire and love.

Fiddler John

Who is this man in the picture,
standing proud and bold?
He was John Brady, a fiddler,
neigh one hundred years old.
Sit down for a wee nip,
and his legend to you I'll unfold.

At just eight years of age,
the fiddle John learned how to play
from his grandfather, who reminded him
to practice every day.
"Perfection, wee'un," he said,
"isn't handed out on a tray."

And so, John grew up to be
the best fiddler in the land,
never promoting himself
nor joining any Irish band.
Was it the way he held his bow
or how he tapped his feet?
No matter, when John fiddled,
it was a musical treat.

For weddings and funerals,
sometimes, he played classical,
but for church, favorite hymns,
something ecclesiastical.
At parties and pubs,
his fingers flew as fast as a jig,
but with the ladies,

an Irish ballad was always big.
Musicians and teachers
from across Europe came
just to hear John play,
and they would applaud
and then enthusiastically say,
"You have no degree.
Still, you're better than we."

Meekly, John would smile and
reply with a voice as sweet as honey,
"Well, you see, I don't play for money
but for God and his people that he loves,
'Cause it's a gift from our Lord up above."

For nearly a century, he fiddled
with all his heart for us all,
and today there still isn't a fiddler
like John Brady that I can recall.
It was on a Saturday, almost midnight,
when John passed away.
He was buried with his fiddle,
in a graveyard overlooking Laugh Neagh.

Irish Santa Clause

Dressed up in his red suit,
he looks really quite cute.
His beard is bright white,
but around his mouth
it's dark brown.
Too much stout he had
at the local pub in town.

Where his skin is exposed,
he looks as red as a rose.
Damp, chilly weather
has caused this, I suppose.
His brogue has a rhythm
like the Westminster chimes.
Invite him to your home
to bring presents and to dine.

For the boys, he will bring
toy cars and peppermint canes,
and maybe, a new bike
by the gate down the lane.
For the girls, he will leave
all kinds of wonderful things:
dolls, clothes, trinkets,
and all sorts of rings.

He is kind-natured
and will show you respect.
Just for his smile and brogue,
you'll welcome him back.

Irish Leek Soup Recipe

1. Dice up six good-sized potatoes
    or a wee bit more,
    unless you want to feed
    more than a score.

2. Put the potatoes in a pot with water
    just over their top.
    Boil until tender,
    and the inside is nice and hot.

3. In a separate pan,
    cook and brown a breast of chicken.
    Then, cut it up tiny.
    Give a piece to the wee dog,
    so he won't get whiney.

4. Cut up two large leeks.
    Make sure the pieces are small.
    Wash out sand and grit, pebbles and all.

5. Chop up some fresh parsley,
    a handful will do.
    Eat a wee bit.
    Then, kiss your sweetheart so true.

6. Add salt and pepper
    and boil chicken and vegetables combined,
    for about ten minutes,
    while you sip on some wine.

7. After leeks, parsley, potatoes, and chicken
are cooked,
stir in two cups of whole milk
and one of heavy cream.
The soup's almost ready
and will taste really keen.

8. Mix in some corn starch or flour
to thicken the soup.
Now you will have just enough
to feed a small group.

Belfast City

In the past, Belfast City, capital of the North of Ireland, has been torn with strife and hate. On the walls, I saw many slogans that depicted hate and the lack of tolerance for church leaders and persecution of people, in general, for their respective beliefs. Hate can come out of the pulpit, as well, and is sometimes taught to the young. Nevertheless, there are also ministers and priests that teach that we really do need to love our neighbours unconditionally.

O God, look down on this divided city.
See the rage, the hate, and the pity.
Regardless of religious view,
only through you can change be true.

Children on their way to school,
for their beliefs, are stoned and ridiculed.
Graffiti on the walls, words of hate:
erase these words, before it's too late.

Obscene names they call each other,
taught by both father and mother.
A city never truly at peace,
it won't come until these divisions cease.

Why not walk with each other hand in hand,
to reflect God's light on this emerald land?
Both Protestant and Catholic well know
God's words of love and peace they must sow.

The Fairy Bush

On Knox's Farm, not far from my family's home in Northern Ireland, there was a fairy bush clump. It consisted of one large bush and several small ones. Stones were around the bushes, so that the farming equipment would not cut them down.

On Knox's Farm, your fairy bush grows,
and when the full moon is out,
you wee fairies wander about.

Near your bush kelly green.
you are not easily seen,
but your soft music I hear,
and your laughter I know,
and to the fairies of Ireland,
I would say hello.

So, I won't cut down your bush
or rip up your stones,
'cause you are so kind, never mean,
as well you do know.

Blasket Island

*For centuries, Blasket Island was home to many Irish families. Now, the cottages
are in ruin, and this lovely wee island is deserted.*

Blasket Island,
almost forgotten, remote,
part of county Kerry,
just off the southern coast.
There is silence
and sadness on her sands:
her people immigrated
to many other lands.
Children's laughter no longer
fills the air:
the cottage walls are broken,
inside bleak and bare.

Wildflowers, grass, and shrubs
still grow,
and visitors to her lonely shores
rarely go.
Her graveyard is filled
with young and old,
of brave Celts who stood
against the Atlantic's cold.

At times, Blasket Island
seems very far away,
but when the mist and the fog lift,
we see and love her a little more each day.

Massacre at Drogheda

Regardless of the spin some historians put on the life and deeds of Oliver Cromwell, he was a madman, full of violence and hate for the Roman Catholic Church and its followers. Cromwell was of Welsh ancestry and of Celtic blood, yet at Drogheda, North of Dublin, he did not hesitate to crush the city and her people.

However, although we may remember what happened, we must show the true love of God, and we must not hate the English or any other past oppressors for what happened. We cannot reclaim the past and make it right. May God give us tolerance and love, regardless of race, religion, or transgressions.

In sixteen-forty-nine,
to Ireland the army of Oliver Cromwell came.
Their hatred for the Irish and Catholics
brought them great fame.
Landing in Dublin,
neigh ten thousand strong,
they marched on Drogheda City -
How shameful! How wrong!

As Cromwell moved towards Drogheda,
along the Boyne River,
the Celts stood their ground,
too angry to quiver.
Ready, willing,
and over two thousand strong,
those Celts fought bravely,
fiercely, and long.

Drogheda stood
in this cruel, bloodthirsty man's way,
and for defiance against his army,
he made her people pay.

CREAMY CELTIC CAKE

He burned the city to the ground.
Mangled corpses everywhere could be found.

Dear God!
Can Cromwell and his men ever be forgiven?
They raped, tortured, and killed
both women and children!
They spilled innocent blood
upon our Irish soil,
then hastily gathered and divided the spoil!

Long gone is the army
of this insane, vicious man,
but we cannot forget
their atrocities on our land,
but from her ashes, Drogheda
is again proud and bold,
reminding us even bitter history
no one can uphold.

Politicians Down Under

There will be honest politicians in heaven.
This we all know,
but too many others will journey
to a place far below,
joining self-righteous Republicans
and shady Democrats,
fitting in with crooked lawyers
and the rest of the rats.

There'll be no mansions
nor second homes by the beach.
To those greedy, elected officials,
it's all out of reach.

No talk of global warming,
no glaciers there down under,
'cause in hell, speaking politics
is just a red hot blunder.

There will be no apple pie, fine wine,
or roast beef or lamb stew.
Those crooks don't even belong
to Satan's chosen few.

One drop of water they will beg for
but cannot even buy.
The devil and his imps will cackle,
when they all sob and cry.

Even in hell,
among the most evil of sinners,
they are a disgrace.
Down under, no promises nor lies
will get them out of that place.

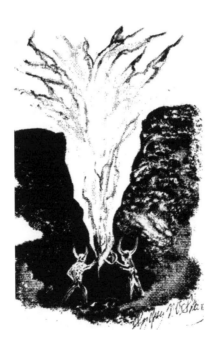

Old Plough Horse

When I was growing up in northwest County Down, a neighbour farmer ploughed with a team of horses and was reluctant to give them up to make way for a tractor.

Jake, the old plough horse,
had green pastures
until he passed away,
replaced by a tractor
farmer Knox bought one early May.

Along the trout stream,
Jake would take a short walk,
drinking the cool water,
pausing only to gaze at the hawks,
and in the winter, he stayed warm in the barn,
treated with respect and dignity throughout the farm.

Yes, farmer Knox loved that old horse
and gave him fine oats and hay,
a loving bond between them
until Jake's final days.

Inspirational Poems

God's Promise

You put the rainbow
in the sky.
Your promise
one cannot deny.
Those seven colors
you blend so well.
It's only you
who can make them gel.

When we see that deep
and awesome red,
we know on the cross
your son has bled.
The orange speaks of
the setting sun
and of our life
with you to come.

The rainbow's prism reflects
the mimosa's yellow,
a sign of peace,
so quiet, so mellow.
The rainbow's green
is soft, and it's light.
It's only you
who makes it just right.

And, of course, the gentle, calm blue
the entire world may see,
and think of him

who has made us all free.
The color indigo
is very rare.
So, it's only he
who can compare.

The violet hue
is a symbol to us,
one of your love
and also your trust.

The silent rainbow
can fade away,
but forever,
your promises will stay.

Highway to Heaven

If you are on life's highway to heaven,
a long, winding road,
don't expect it to be paved
with silver or gold.
There'll be mountains upon mountains
rugged and steep,
but at the end of your journey,
the Lord you shall meet.

On the highway to heaven,
Jesus walks each step of the way,
and the sunshine of his presence
turns your darkness into day.

God sees each wide river and ravine
you must carefully cross.
Keep your eyes focused on him,
and you won't stray or get lost.

The road is paved with God's love.
His son, on the way, died on the cross,
for you and me in a world full of sin,
a cruel world, misguided and lost.

At the end is a city of light,
built in heaven, at least four square.
The redeemed of all faiths stand together,
with God's presence everywhere.

Irish Farmer's Prayer

Before you now,
O Lord, I pray,
"Oh, please help me
with my corn and my hay.

My tired, sore back
is growing weak,
and so, through you,
your strength I must seek.

Please help me to love
both friend and foe.
Forgive me if ever I have
wronged you so.

Your son, he's the sunshine
of my soul.
Please, always keep me
within your fold.

I thank you now
for this lush soil and land.
God, I love you and will serve you
as much as I can."

Inspiration

Behold the rocky spires and peaks
that rise from the desert floor below.
They are the inspirations
to my soul.

No need to enter into worship
through a massive, ornate door,
'cause my altar may be a rock
on the rugged mountainside
or a stone upon the sandy, desert floor.

Christ had no mansion here,
no place to call his home,
often walking hot desert paths,
very lonely and quite alone.

At times, his canopy
was the moon and stars above,
his body, the temple,
always filled with truth and love.

The Lord dwells within us,
not in structures made by man,
yet some church leaders don't see this truth,
not wanting nor trying to understand.

No matter the view,
as we walk life's winding path,
may God with us be,

through green meadows and jagged rocks
and along the soft shores of the raging sea.

Thoughts

A thought about our America,
our land of the free,
filled with great kindness,
God certainly sees.

High in the Rockies,
a pristine meadow
below a gentle waterfall
reminds me of God:
His peace and goodness
that we hold in perfect awe.

The meadow's wildflowers,
with their beauty and
perfumes so sweet,
remind me in God's heaven,
someday, we shall meet.

That thought about heaven
is a delightful, special thing,
bringing peace and joy,
so it makes us sing.

And the Lord himself,
like whirling windmills
when the invisible wind
moves their blades –
we don't see Him,
but his love never fades.

Our thoughts: may they always be
uplifting and good,
because, to our souls,
they are the most perfect food.

Speak Words

Mothers:
Speak to your unborn child
words of our Lord,
pure and undefiled.

Speak words of love,
of joy, and of peace,
bringing strength to others,
and your faith shall increase.

Speak to the stranger
you meet on life's highway.
He could be an angel
you will know again someday.

Speak words that praise God.
Thank him for his son,
from the dawn throughout the day
and past the setting sun.

Tree of Destiny

Unnoticed by man,
a small seedling grew
in our Father's sight,
always in his plain view.
Rain, sunshine, and God's love
made the little tree grow,
but it didn't know where
it would finally go.

As the years went by,
it grew thick, tall, and strong,
planted out of love,
for a world gone so wrong.
The wood from the tree
created our dear Savior's cross,
carried up Calvary's hill
for sinners eternally lost.

Our Savior looked down,
nailed to the wood from the tree,
knowing he lived and died
for sinners like me.
The blood-stained wood
has long rotted to dust,
but in God's perfect plan,
we always can trust.

Eternal Love

As God's children,
we are given pure love,
coming down unfiltered
from heaven above.

Purchased by gold,
it just cannot be.
For those who will seek him,
it's willing and free.

Free to us all,
for our Savior has risen.
It's in God's plan
and needs no revision.

He has promised us mansions
when our work here is done,
from him, our loving God,
and from Jesus, his son.

So, love one another,
despite religion or race,
and we'll be in heaven,
beyond outer space.

The Last Bridge

There is but one last bridge
that we all must cross,
between God's Earth
and his heaven across.

The bridge will be as clear as crystal
morning, evening, and night;
no more horizons,
'cause there we'll be
in God's eternal light.

We will need
neither fine compass nor maps
to point us the way.
His angels will guide us o'er the bridge
that last beautiful day.

At this bridge to eternity,
there'll be no toll to pay.
We'll be able to cross over
without any delay.

Our passport is signed:
Forever we can stay.
We will see peace and joy
on all those faces we'll meet,
who'll be 'ever worshiping
with the Lord at his feet.

Others' Shoes

If I walked in others' shoes,
how much more would I
understand and appreciate?

If I walked in a blind man's shoes,
I would miss the spring wildflowers,
their powerful purples and yummy yellows,
the rustic reds of autumn,
and the effervescent orange of the twilight sky
no artist can truly duplicate.

If I walked in a deaf man's shoes,
I would never hear the ever-changing music
of the mountain stream,
or the hoot of the big-horned owl
on a misty ridge nearby,
and the rolling thunder introducing
the welcome, soft rain upon my face.

If I walked in a dumb man's shoes,
I would long to give thanks to my parents,
in my own voice,
for their unwavering love,
or to tell children stories
of noble knights defending
their princesses and castles,
or above all, to speak joyfully to God
of my humble gratitude for all that he is.

Beyond

Don't cry and weep
when I am gone,
but give praise to God
in joyful song.
My soul will soar as an eagle
to the utmost height,
and I will fearlessly fly
into God's eternal light.

I will leave behind
this old Earth
full of sin and sorrow
and enter into heaven,
where I know
there's a bright tomorrow.
My passport has been made ready
by Christ's death upon the cross,
and for all of us
who believe in him,
none will be lost.

So, just lift your voice towards heaven
in praise and in song,
and know
that within his arms
and to him I belong.

Made in the USA
Charleston, SC
19 December 2012